HER
RED HAIR
RISES
WITH THE
WINGS OF
INSECTS

HER RED HAIR RISES WITH THE WINGS OF INSECTS

— POEMS —

CATHERINE GRAHAM

WOLSAK
& WYNN

Book design: Natalie Olsen, Kisscut Design
Author photograph: Prosopon Photography
Typeset in Miller, Trade Gothic and Missionary
Printed by Coach House Printing Company Toronto, Canada

Canada Council   Conseil des Arts
for the Arts   du Canada

Canadian   Patrimoine
Heritage   canadien

ONTARIO ARTS COUNCIL
CONSEIL DES ARTS DE L'ONTARIO

50 YEARS OF ONTARIO GOVERNMENT SUPPORT OF THE ARTS
50 ANS DE SOUTIEN DU GOUVERNEMENT DE L'ONTARIO AUX ARTS

The publisher gratefully acknowledges the support of the Canada Council
for the Arts, the Ontario Arts Council and the Canada Book Fund.

Wolsak and Wynn Publishers Ltd.
280 James Street North
Hamilton, ON
Canada L8R 2L3

Library and Archives Canada Cataloguing in Publication

Graham, Catherine, author
Her red hair rises with the wings of insects / Catherine Graham.

Poems.
ISBN 978-1-894987-76-9 (pbk.)

I. Title.

PS8563.R31452H47 2013   C811'.6   C2013-905446-4

for John Coates

and in memory of Dorothy Molloy and P. K. Page

#

Most of the poems in this book began as glosas, an early Renaissance form developed during the fourteenth century by poets in the Spanish court. The opening four lines of another poet's work (the cabeza) are woven into the last line of each of four ten-line stanzas.

In my last book, *Winterkill*, one of the poems, "The Buried," was nearly a glosa. I had woven a quote from actor Tilda Swinton into the last lines of six stanzas. Until this poem, most of my work had been shorter; usually fewer than ten lines, but the glosa format demanded more of me. After *Winterkill* was published I wondered if I could write another poem like "The Buried" but this time a true glosa. With countless poetry books in my study to choose from, it was *Gethsemane Day* by the late Irish poet Dorothy Molloy I pulled off the shelf. Without giving it too much thought, I chose four lines that spoke to me and began.

There was no plan, just an instinct to try writing a form I was familiar with from reading the glosas of P. K. Page. With several attempts under my belt I gave myself a mission: to write a glosa using a cabeza from each of Molloy's poems in *Gethsemane Day*.

When this process ended I wanted more, so I reached for Molloy's first posthumous book, *Hare Soup* (Molloy died ten days before this book was published by Faber and Faber), and although I didn't write as many glosas as I did with *Gethsemane Day* a few came into being.

After letting the glosas sit I found a fresh and lively energy; a feeling of lyricism often coupled with a sinister edge, but sometimes it felt like the format was getting in the way.

I began to listen to the demands of each poem by letting go of the poem's initial scaffolding. Yet, despite the partial or complete erasure of Molloy's lines, they were essential to my process.

I lived in Northern Ireland during the 1990s but never met Molloy. I did meet P. K. Page in 2006 when she invited me to her home in Victoria, British Columbia. She was a gracious, sharp-witted, inspiring host during an afternoon that went by too quickly. It was a visit I cherish.

Dorothy Molloy and P. K. Page became my spirit mentors during the writing of *Her Red Hair Rises with the Wings of Insects*. This book is my tribute to them.

Catherine Graham
July 2013
Toronto

THE GOOD POET
WELDS HIS THEFT
INTO A WHOLE
OF FEELING
WHICH IS UNIQUE,
UTTERLY DIFFERENT
FROM THAT FROM
WHICH IT WAS TORN.
—T. S. ELIOT

TO THE ANIMAL HE MET IN THE DARK

I've often thought about you.

How you came in the night, in the middle of the night,
to stand on the road for some goddamn reason.

How in the blinding light you stood as still as branches,
like anything trapped.

Nothing to see in the darkened windshield—
just the last expression on my drunk father's face,

and you, white-tailed beast, reflected, just like that,
on your way through your own nocturnal route.

I have so often thought about you.

CHTHONIC

The lilacs have risen to solo in the corner orchestra of greens.
Purple odours permeate the branched alveoli of my lungs.
I slip through the briars, listen to wind shaking the canopy, stand
in place till I'm pulled through the port of entry.

I fight. Play possum. But my wit leaks as lilacs rust
from bone ivory. Death seeps. I hold
my breath to tease the light they say is coming,
but like *the trees I* darken *the forest.*

You must find the hidden passage inside the earth's purse.
Chewing worms. Burrowing owls! Nothing is still,
not even my mind turning to brain, a field in fallow. The earth
slides over my face. I see the exchange that's happening—

a dead mother wants out. Her red hair rises with the wings
of insects, and I sink further than *the lair of the fox.*

after "The Woman and the Hill" **Hare Soup**

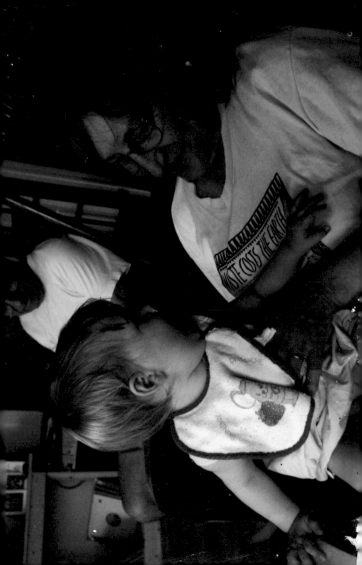

GOLD CARP

Mint, weed and stone. Black water takes the night down
and darkness is held a hostage, a trap.

I think of the fish that swam in the quarry's inlet—
shallow pocket barred with light.

I never cared for fish but *I was quite fond of one.*
Torpedo gold. As still as the drowned floats alone.

Cornered for no reason. No aquarium as cage or
wall as trap. No toes to dip. No liquid to cup.

A hunch-backed carp, he used to raise my mood
when he mouthed the bread pellets.

Our images met at the hinge of our worlds.
Bottom-feeder. Bottomless sun.

READING

He's not done yet—
He tightens the rope and drops
his voice into my *chest. I endure;*
stare through closed dreams
I haven't slept through yet—

Mouth tuned to the rhythm of a voice box
poet man needs no dais to look tall
to his locked-in audience.
I feel *half-naked, my pelvis exposed*
between the lines of each stanza.

Clouds shift to receive new registers.
Criss-crossed on my lap, *my hands* swell
as the room thins. I know what
happens happens—Him in me
circling like a wolf.

WINTER BROCCOLI

Not for the backdrop, but to enter green.
How should I place my foreign foot?
Already this land unlikens me. Blood-soaked
drumlins. The Antrim accent makes my inner ear *bleed*.

Oh, but the purrs of a pub in strings.
His voice slips through my sixth sense.
Medicinal split between this and this.
And he is so real. And I am so normal.

Purple hearts sprouting flowers in hedgerows carry
the glisten of sex as the night blows stars to deafen
our ears and we are safe beside the sea's deep
negotiations, *unseen in the forests of* our own taking.

I pine no more. My home is his skin.
But the ocean can't hold without Earth as container,
Moon as pull. No oxygen in ether. Only stars
that fail to shape this *winter broccoli*.

after "Four Haikus" Gethsemane Day

VOW OF THE GROUNDED TONGUE

In my mind I don't make the vow. Slip a stuffed horse
in my bed, make its head my head under the cotton sheets.

Night serves to even out misaligned shapes—*so I dress,*
slip the latch like an accomplished thief, go out the back door,
left unlocked. The house, a storm stay of sleep with me not in it.

Slumbering dreams float up the chimney's lip like ghosts
pining for skin. I *make my way down* the long gravel driveway,
past shadows of rabbits and shut-eyed birds; black trees shift

in dark shudders. The moon teases: I see you as I ascend
the stairs. At the click of the latch to your king-sized room—there,
curved in sleep, like the stuffed horse hiding my shape.

One lost self finds another as you rise, a crescent grin on your face,
and pat the place we know I'll fit. The click *of stiletto on marble.*

after "Live Model" Gethsemane Day

BETWEEN HIS FINGER & HIS THUMB

The way the sun peeks out from a continent
of cloud, a geyser of light that rams the sea
and breaks all meaning into knuckling diamonds,
he gave me full instructions re *weather* once he knew
what I needed to know. Dumb as a round square,
I sat there while he sped the car over green hills,
the bleating sheep too fat to be clouds, too warm
to be snow. We rode through a tunnel of rock,
blasted to give route—back and forth each *season,*
light cloud cover over the sea. Always the clouds, even
at night. But the moon pushed the bloom
of the ivory in waves that rippled less than diamonds,
more like the glow of a spotlight we felt when we did
what we did, and the round moon entered and
took us in, like *the sun at an angle like this he showed me,*
and I believed him, even though he wore the evidence
of ceremony. But what's a band of hollow gold?
A ringless moon or a sun eaten by dark circles.
We saw the dark circles; we were the dark circles,
but who can see when the night is strung (between
his finger and thumb) and the sky just like that.

after "How to see Wales" Gethsemane Day

RIVERBED

I shudder to think that I once needed
the intervention of reason. The V of my lap
tingled *along the bikini-line* where he opened me up
like a riverbed, the sheets surrounded
by sand and the rapid waves we made
beside the sea's flat rock that *yielded fibroids*
of moisture and moss. We grew a life
beneath the blanket. We fell like fruit after
August rain, pearling the dew of the aftermath.
Our rind, our doubling, *big as melons.*

after "Fruits of the Womb" Gethsemane Day

CLOAK

I hide my power in a cloak I hoard as anger.
My jaw gears like a charging bull;
hairs horn from my butting forehead.

Stick of flame, I bring fresh heat
to a room like sun in *sky. There is no edge
from which to hang* your escape. I whore surrender.

Not bad, this giving up. No tit
for tat just a hit in the chest
where you slip between heartbeats.

Mushroom mouth.

Don't say I don't share *my plumb-line. No ledge
on which to lay* your lost self? Give in
to my configuration. Hang on to a happy organ.

Be good and be dummy spewing out of my mouth.
Sing sweetly to *my spirit-level. And you are outside
piling logs* for relief. Even hunger needs a break.

Now let's pretend you're mad again. Committed
to a door with no handles; marionette strings
sting sharp injections.

And you'll keep coming back
because I keep you
working on your own wreckage.

TCHOTCHKES

He says he'll write. Sometimes he does with letters so spare
and spiny like cacti they sting the absence.

I wait like a child for more tchotchkes from other countries
where air floats cobalt blue or hot vermilion.

If I could trap his taste on my tongue, I'd keep it boxed
like *a doll from Bogotá.*

All I have are hands with river etches that map his exotic locales,
and this rock where I outline *a fossil of fish* to carve his story.

Only my hand under water, the swan-tilt
of my wrist, *a bangle from Arabia—*

He's always leaving me and telling me he's coming back.
"Soon," he says, pointing to the moon.

But when it's full or empty?
He doesn't answer. He says he'll write.

after "Queen's Ransom" Gethsemane Day

TOURNIQUET

Nobody can say she can't beat him on the tennis court.
Her shots land safely on lines and chalk flies up in puffs
of surrender, but take him home and he's the official.

His whistle lives inside his mouth between the pink
of his teeth. Like a drawbridge she lowers *on a string,*
makes waves at the moat she can no longer cross.

Come back, come pull her up. She can't straighten herself
in her flattened state or feel his foot pumping her back.
She can't see a thing until he signals: over.

Cotton is cover—what clothes are for, and hair that falls
across forehead and shoulders. She knows the pain
a hospital hides like the red on her arm now blue now white.

She'll *make a tourniquet* out of his next attack. Then
one day he leaves. She is lying on the floor even though
she's standing up in the house of herself. Cornered, quiet.

DOMESTIC

He sculpts my words with the chisel of his mouth.
Fits me inside his mind's binding. I do what I'm told
to get my playpen back, the edge of no to end
each *day. What did I do* to exit his eyes?
Blue-blinding marbles detached from the brain
that stems them. He won't answer. Sits
in his fat easy chair. What did I do *or what
did I do not* but wear something pretty? He spits
his words in blurry circles; hurls stones
of vowels at fields of bruises. Clothes
with round edges give too much of me to see.
"Who you trying to impress? Some fancy man?"
He's laughing now. "You think I'm serious? Just
want you to be safe, Pet." Blind *heart, pack up and run.*

RING-NECKED

I am aproned to his kitchen. Calico
and gingham print. My lap
is his garden. My back, a tied string.
I make the pots boil, bring steam
to his table. Flower the walls with spice.

He shoves hot oats into his slot, chews
like a foregone conclusion. "Your bloody
dog's in that bowl." I shake his red leash.

"Very funny," he says as he exits the table.
The cushion, cupped with the imprints
of his buttocks. They melt away. They
always do. But the ring round his neck—

HAT RABBIT

She left us waiting for the rabbit in the hat. How long
do you stare at a black top hat waiting for a rabbit
to hop out?   She was like our mother
for seven years. She never responds to our calls.
The blood that runs through us doesn't match;
we can't signal her homing.   *They* say she *left*
because our Dad wasn't nice. The neighbours leave *us*
grief trees in their stares; we see the pity seeding their eyes.
So tempting to scoop the jelly out.   Or better yet,
to tap it like sap. Poor little orphans. We aren't orphans.
We have a father and a file of postcards, so we know
where she is: *wailing at the wall* in a distant country.
Magic isn't a trick. It's the return of
what you want. *And that was all.*

after "Death by poisoning" Gethsemane Day

CROWN ISLAND

I am surrounded by Crown Island,
a weave of rock and sand; the waves
lap against me, sizzling white strings.

On my head sits the appointed crown,
stapled and fastened, now part of my mind.
My earrings of polished tin

take in the sun, moon, rain.
Each mirrored wave of a wave under water.
Someone must see to the world below.

I ask the sky. I *flash at the Northern Lights,*
twisting their capes like kaleidoscopes.
Black clouds cloud the black.

I shovel up the sea to check beneath the blue.
I'm looking for white wounds.
The cold is quick. Quick, enter me.

after "Ice Maiden" Hare Soup ⊢ 15 ⊣

YOU ARE DEAD TO ME

No more high windows
brittled from rain.

Now I remember
the sweet names of things:

roses, carnations,
camellias, begonias.

No more brick of you
to weigh me down in the cellar

where darkness shot roots
through *the stems of* my ankles.

after "Trophy" **Gethsemane Day**

FLIES GATHER

There is much agony in the entrails of love.
I breathe the way your paintings breathe.
You walk ahead as the rain nails down.
Clouds need release.
Those long cotton pods by the side of the road...
You enter the dusk of your painting.
I become the lost colour you float above.
Remember us?
Go ahead, frown.
Pull out my tongue from the root of my mouth. Then
love me again till *the sickle moon cuts.*
Love me again till *the sickle moon cuts.*
Pull out my tongue from the root of my mouth. Then
go ahead, frown.
Remember us?
I become the lost colour you float above.
You enter the dusk of your painting.
Those long cotton pods by the side of the road...
Clouds need release.
You walk ahead as the rain nails down.
I breathe the way your paintings breathe.
There is much agony in the entrails of love.

GATHER FLIES

COUCH

He tells me desire is away from your stars.
His corset to keep *my third eye ablaze.*
He tightens my girth to the wind-down hour.
That look on his face. He sees what I think.

after "Stigmata" **Hare Soup**

INSIDE THE STORM'S EYE

Not everyone wants to go
to the storm's eye. Cat
has made our lawn a field
of blood-flecked rabbit. The tap
is still running, *the waters*
are overflowing—Mother
closes the curtains.
The in-ground nest you
fingered (yesterday?):
a feral scene.
                    Make believe
won't bring those babies back. No
squirms left *to subside. The creatures*
in my cranium increased that night—
sores oozed between long ears
and cold eyes—trickling
like a nutty tap until that
last attempt at pipe-tightening—look
at the neighbour's cat—
can't think: kitty. Nice kitty. No.
Think: squeeze hand—Think: push
the domestic out—seeing bloodstained teeth—
The mean in me bred *and multiplied.*

after "Life Boat" Gethsemane Day

ACHE

So cold, so dry, where is
the echo of my echo?

The umbilical cord
is cut and I'm pure.

Never so.

Father's ears. Mother's brow.
What is said to my future is:

"Isn't she?"
I miss my slip of water.

THE CALLING

Cedar walls keep good company.

Lidless eyes never leave me bereft.

Night is pinned with eyes, too.

I jigsaw the Fates—I won't

come out to the zigzagging *bats*.

I join the points to map my new myth.

But *the wolves rush by in packs*.

Their soft howls of smoke—

I'm wanted on all fours.

THE ANIMAL GAME

Now I'm a bird in the nest of your lap.
I flap my blanket of feathers.
Elongate my growing neck.

You take another one out, and I leap:
frog-green and slippery,
my tongue slides, ruler-long—

I aim for your fingers. You pretend
to dribble and present it to me.
It roughens my tongue like wolf teeth.

We feel the drumming tremble. Mean fists.
Our game is bruised.
Sit down. Your grandmother's coming.

PLAITS

When tomorrow is today, our kitchen turns salon
with my hair bowed over the sink. Once air-dried,
you twist it into rings like yarn wound round a pencil.
"Stay." And like a good dog it does. "You're Shirley
Temple now." Come Sunday, when Nana visits,
you wind it in a chignon. "Grace Kelly." "Who?"
I ask as you pull at the curls, tight as the circles

in a Spirograph. My hair is braided through your hands.
Grown-up hands, ringed with time and growth,
like the rings you carry in the quiet girth of your bones.
"Hold still." Grasses river from my scalp. They catch
the August air like sweat on tennis freckles. "When
you trap your mop in plaits, you are braiding back
to your own childhood." The ends twist to fishhooks.

after "Crowning Glory" Gethsemane Day

THE BULLIED

When I play invisible, the boy
sneers. I look away
and he's still looking.
His gathering of buddies
mock me with their yawn-traps.
You must learn how to look
and look back.

Can they see me now
when I press against the red brick wall
as they play Planet of the Apes?
I'm the lost thought inside the ocean
in Mrs. Easy's atlas.
How I'm gyred through the ether
is how God made me.

We are all icebergs to turn
green inside. Clouds hang
at half-mast. Another mother
is dying. The sun screams
yellow until the ding
of the recess bell. I fall in line.
Can they see in this stalk of wild fennel,

the twinkle of my silver buckle?
Big feet, they snigger.
I feel dot small. The crayon wave
on my paper rides the hair of water.
The scent of chalk is not home.
You pay a price when the cat's got your tongue.
Fire in the face, the cinder *and spark.*

after "Freed Spirit" **Gethsemane Day**

JAMAICA

I had two dolls to give away and kept both.
Black faces of Jamaica, sponges
of soft cloth, sunny colours of Ocho Rios.

Hide what you hoard, and invisible pins
grow inside you. At night in bed,
stretched out along its length, I listened to the inward

guilt gnawing at the pink lining,
small animal teeth. Too late.
I've been home now for weeks.

Stuffed them in the back of the drawer
so they won't be seen when my friends come
to play. The *hesitation of its bells, the angel voices*

have turned into devils. God knows
what you did. He orchestrates the midnight
gnawing. Now they're too ugly to play with.

Bright hues—sick, fruit rancid.
They bring black flies to the room.
Rising from the choir behind the screen, they buzz

back and forth and wait
for me to open that drawer
to land as pennies on eyes.

Smell the pickling stink of the dump
where garbage merges and no God hears
the organ-music pumping through my bones.

after "I spend the night" Gethsemane Day

PEAS & BARBIES

Make her naked and still she smiles,
exposing breasts without nipples.

Nipple.

We giggled at the word in the secret book
where the small arrow pointed.

Nipple.
We said it at the same time.

I made a doll of mashed potato
with nipple-peas on my plate.

Take charge *and spit.*
Witless move. Nana's looking.

Don't play with your food says the line
in her lips that melts the wizard in mine.

She blinks the nippled world away.
I give the world too much.

Fork more food in your mouth
and keep your eyes shut;

be an *empty-headed thing*
with shredded carrot hair.

Now roll on into Vegetable Land
where potatoes rule and peas shrivel

when told to stack up like tennis balls
on a Prince racquet.

Which one will tip the hill?
This pea. That.

"Eat your meal. It's getting cold.
You'll be hungry later."

I'll chew my *hair*.

"Nipple."

CERAMIC

Knick-knacks entice. Touch, and she won't forgive.

She knows what you are. Sweet on the tongue.

Can't hide plum pudding from fruitcake.

A good cook knows her ingredients. Cedar boughs

fit indoors and ribbons glisten. The nativity scene

shines its light *through the drip* of another candle.

Camels unfurl their black lips, hovering over the blessed manger,

and the stiff baby cries in ceramic. Now black is a crack below

blue-robed Mary who screams she'll *eat* your *hair with fluorescent teeth.*

AT THE SATURDAY MATINEE

The projector lights up the dark to its half-self.
Yet I don't feel his touch until his hand slips
through *my blouse*. What this man wants

no one's had, not even the boys in my head.
I kick him aside before slipping through a curtain
to the closest door—a room with no room.

When I stab at the O of his mouth with my fist,
his tooth shoots out like a touch-me-not.
Under my foot like a pebble. A man

with my sharp-pointed penknife waves
his flashlight at my face. "Show's over," he says.

after "Hare Soup" Hare Soup

SMALL HIDDEN DOOR

Before image comes something else.

A stalking wind that
turns visible through a dark keyhole.

A man moves helter-skelter without moving his feet,
like a child's toy—

here, now here, now closer like a mouth
opening and closing, opening and closing—

to a small hidden door,
to the smell of gamey meat.

JELLY-BEAN

Now that he knows he can use his hands as hers—
that crush of attention snakes June through her winter skin,
makes minnows sun-flip through her stomach.

He *wished himself dead when he ate out her heart,*
but that's when she was beneath his moist sounds.

The thrum of his uncle blood quickens the trick
of the mind into a moan as *small as a jelly-bean.*
So small, they all refused to believe it.

BLACK WEEDS

Black weeds invade

smooth pink fields.

She did not plant them.

She does not want their

warm curls. At night

she dreams they leap,

and are never happy

staying home. Things

that shouldn't be,

are (as they should

be). Black weeds

and not pink fields.

after "Was it like this?" **Hare Soup**

PETALS

Wrapped in the soft palate cloth of her throat,
her roughly smooth voice has gingered red,

and her palatine uvula hangs stiff as a stalactite,
as small as a finger without the half-moon nail.

It hangs useless and trapped as a fired trapeze man
and so unlike the deep roots she keeps burying—

the fractal limbs of the fragile plants and spring
flowers: the begonias, petunias. The rose. For what

emerges, emerges slowly despite the dead heading.
She sees her fruits lift from each finger-pinch,

and what emerges slowly grows between her soil-
covered legs into a ring of pink volcanoes.

THE QUEEN IS NOT WELCOME HERE

She won't leave, the Queen. She is hogging
my room, my living room. She is waiting
for me to leave my bedroom. And Bobby Orr
keeps waiting by the door, tapping his
hockey stick—a clock, a trick—Get out! I won't.

I cradle myself in my sheets, *the blood
I am sweating rubs off...* I hear the "Pomp
and Circumstance" playing outside
my chair-jammed door. She is hungry now,
her Majesty. I sense it for the brass has stopped.

Her growls slip through the doorway slit,
quick pink contractions. I grab for the phone.
I holler: I'm coming! *but I'm still holding
on to my head* between the sheets. It hurts
even more with this receiver at my ear.

"They won't leave," I say to my daughter.
"Calm down, Mother. I'm coming over."
And the music starts up again to the tapping stick,
and the Avenger is waiting in his bowler hat,
his brelly's a tock to Bobby Orr's tack.

What cocktail is Daddy preparing for me? When
will my daughter open the door? I hear
my lost youth in her questioning voice.
I peek out the front—she is tossing a bag
down the garbage chute. I hear the long slide.

"Say goodbye to them, Mother." I won't. I can't.

after "Gethsemane Day" Gethsemane Day

ASYLUM WALL

The warehousing of the mad
began with wooden walls
the year of John A's birth.

In 1860, wood turned brick
from patient labour.

Robin and sparrow now mock
our locked-in state.

Sky flit like that *Jack Rabbit*—
shoulder blades are useless wings.

Still, some of us escape.

Easier in trousers. Skirts like bells
weigh you down. And with money

to be had for our capture, we keep
coming back like the rats that never leave.

That hungry one is gnawing
a hole in my skull.

It's no use living anymore.

Here.   Francis.   1891.

I'm dust.

TOO MUCH LIGHT

"Too much light can kill," says Philomena,
pulling her dog bouquet across the shady park.
A charge of blossoms blows down

and *the world's* an *undone* puzzle. Too
much light? Think of praise
raining. Words that matter

make you more than you are, the way *money*
triggers a cashier's ka-ching! And happy molecules
jewel new orbits of silent flies.

I am the light and *sin is gone. It's all elastic* anyhow.
Not raisin stiff on a windowsill. We move
forward to bend and catch our past...

She is pointing at my face—the mark. The dogs
sniff. "Say it! Say what you mean!" *Philomena's
hesitating*: "Sun on the skin, unprotected."

THE NIGHT PRAYER'S LORD

If I should wake before I die, I'll be in a box. I'll be
in the dark. I'll need a bell to ring—Oh, let me
be Victorian. My breath on glass. The wet stone
in your hand. Help me out of this coffin. Don't
let the woodworms in. Listen for the trapline going
knock knock. Help! Or *I'll take that beam out of my eye*
by cracking the oak. Let second chance surge
through me like a Greek chorus—Saggy skin,
droopy eyelids, blue-veined hands, dryness
between legs, the nameless faces—*I'll sail a boat.*
I'll learn to fly! Reactivate adrenalin! Reap
the sown seed! Make life fit into the tunnel I have left.
Do all the things you don't do until the one day
there's nothing to do inside this massive oven.

SNOWFALL

The snow holds light. Winter spins
into a trance. The sky can't keep up
with the falling. The sifting

edges in waves to the roof below the *pitch*
of night the white shoots up.
Ironed moon. Smooth as the dew

hidden in each flake, each crystal imprint
of pedigree lace. *Safe from the world, I hid
there all alone, till suddenly*, I'm falling—

pores—flakes—riding the white drift;
spin calm into a bleach explosion.
I stutter under the gathering spell and wait

for pain to level things out—
the weight of an animal's foot—
dark stirrings are welcome then.

after "Life Boat" Gethsemane Day

VOLUME

Music looking for sound begins in silence.
She carried silence through the grace of our house;
carried her husband's talk, the silent place of his words
that stick like the alphabet magnets infesting the fridge—

letters a child needs to read through the silence.
I never heard her softly un*wrap* what she kept
fisted in her heart's lub-dub, lub-dub, lub-dub,
the red answer for the pump that stretched
oxygenated ribbons of air like *the sea around her,*
an underground current she carried from room to room—

silence that fell *like a shroud*, a tape of unsaid words.
Some of us are born for the hush of the seashell.
What to do when the quarry's uproar calls for us?
I refuse to be her silence. *My life* is *just too loud.*

after "S.O.S." Gethsemane Day

TORPOR

Water holds sky in its face.
No wind-scars of white.

Green beneath
each fish jump.

Everything moves out
of something and

back in again, like falling
leaves through a craze

of *empty skies, only the cries*
that bring the birds back

carry the absence
we can't find.

I want more green
but the quarry grows

a lid, a locked harbour
gripping all

I can't have;
every buried

echo from afar, of some
strange cry that can't get out.

Clothed in cold,
the falling snow

buries the ice,
a blank oval.

But see? Fox tracks,
rabbit, deer and crow

no longer navigating
by a magnetic line,

not everything follows
the *flapping bird.*

STRAWBERRIES

No god smiles on sidewalk cracks around the quarry.
Only fossils like moles and freckles can shape a face
from rock. Tattoo curves are permanent.

Let my touch slip time between these *wild strawberries*
I picked for him in the goldenrod field.
Plump-ripe heads drank the sun into reddening.

Don't stuff so many in your mouth. But who
can resist? As poppies in a field, these *fairy*
berries are *a crop* of how much I love my father.

My tongue can move no language for that.

So I pick wild berries to soften the loss;
the one we no longer have; the dead red hue
that lives in the living-room silence.

I filled a whole thimble, right to the tip
of my thumb where her thumb used to sit
like a head in a hat, safe from needles.

The sewing is silent in her nook.
Clothes are store bought now. No hands
like hers. A thimble's just *a silver container.*

DOG IS MR. LEVENTHAL

She is sleeping with a dog in my dream, when the dog
morphs into Mr. Leventhal. His old body, the meaty
grey of an elephant's, rolls over her and her bedsores

that smell of the mince she's slipping into, that will not
heal like the *red gash in my side* that isn't there when I awake.
Poke the tender spot. What else wants to eat us?

We, walking meals for mosquitoes, the land of honeyed blood
for sword-like *sea creatures with webbed feet* that swim
in the concoction we came from. What makes her hold

onto pain? Every gold trophy glows inside her bones now.
She knows where the finish line is, lying in her hospital bed
that sits inside our house. A finish line of tape *and ductless eyes*

can't help but beckon. No dog or Mr. Leventhal
can seduce her back, only the folds in my brain where
everything shows up in wandering dreams.

FOREST OF SLEEP

I know it's still there, he thinks as the rain
simmers on his fevered head, wet as the cloth
Mamma put there, now dry as a leaf on the carpet.

A boy of twelve lies fast asleep dreaming
for no reason, until he hears: stay still,
stay put. His body twitches, wants out.

To be of no mind is to be a lost country,
tethered to air that's already empty.
He is summoned in dream to stop his heart.

So he falls like a leaf, a curled autumn cloth.
You die when you land, you never wake up.
His eyes scan right to left inside his lids.

He aches *to go to Mamma.* She lies
in a room where the eyes never close.
A felled tree in a forest, the artery of heartwood.

after "Crazy for another baby" Gethsemane Day

THE FIX

What I came out of isn't there anymore. Surgeons
removed the red space. Another part of her
lifted up. Left breast. Then right. And now the cells
aim for the pancreas. *This time they won't scour*
or scrape, only take like greedy mouths. We are all
soft bombs. Pocket watch to wrist. The glass face
stares up and *the womb* is gone. I'm teenaged
and forever homeless. You must enter the ache.
When I say you, I mean I. There is no language for this.
Just clocks that tick and tick, too straight to be a pulse.
Damn the red ache. Take on the line of logic and
flatten it *with the spoon-shaped curette;* accept each
rehearsal of her disappearing act. The essence of her
nesting out of herself. Hold the water of those eyes.
You'll see your quarry. Black pools will flatten to white.

after "Curette" Gethsemane Day

THE CARNIVAL IS COMING

Nobody falls down to signal it's finished.
Her hand is in my mind now, warm
like the coat no longer there and though

she exists in a world of birds, *once
again I'm huddled in my childhood coat,
red* as winter on my cheeks.

Pulled by her hand, we float through the snow
by the icicle garden, where legs, quickened by ice,
match the moon's chalk with *velvet.*

So clap for the barker in the carnival ring
*tightly belted at the waist, and bow before
the sanctuary* of this cold space. The barker

knows he can't be any more real than this
slip of memory through my red velvet coat:
the sun, the centre, the dying red *lamp.*

after "Dream" Gethsemane Day

A MIDNIGHT KNOCK, A SHUDDER

Two wild irises soiled
in the sand of the same seed.

She hides the pain in her apron.
He disappears into the blue vault.

He holds the blue of her eyes,
but wants the brown of his father's.
His glare reopens her scars.

It's then that she bakes bread
from the fruit made to blacken.

Where is he? Where is her son?
A midnight knock, a shudder.

PAIL AND SHOVEL

His last memory was his first.
Pail and shovel on a beach.
Red in a net taken out.

They drove to the ocean that lapped
his last visit and by evening's end—
his convertible disappearing.

You *sit for hours* beneath the dripping taps
in the white and narrow bath trying
to dilute your father's neglect.

Questions trickle as the water
beads down. Oh! *I must needs
have my ablutions.*

You're no longer an only.
A landscape seeds you
to a man you don't recognize.

Pail and shovel on a beach.
Red in a net
taken out.

Salt in the water won't
lessen the evidence.
What makes a father leave?

There is no *solution.*
With hands flapping, water lapping,
a letter leads to a buried memory.

Red in a net.
Pail and shovel on a beach.
Sand through the *silver benedictions from the taps.*

PLOT

On the hill they form families.

Gardens of bone, skin-infested

grasses, fields of buried organs

for the placement of plastic. *Angels*

who freeze won't last—It's colder

than snow in the mausoleum

where the fresh rest *on their plinths*

waiting f*or the Kingdom*—never

to come. But minds that lived

kindly will sprout yellow flowers—

gold *slung down from the sun.*

after "Deansgrange" Gethsemane Day

QUARRY

Blasted   stone-gutted   re-puzzled rock

crossing the Peace Bridge   and never

          coming back   the drowned oval

stocked with fish that lay their eggs next

          to weedy machinery   Quarry

What He sees   when I swim your water

     Sky light defines what He takes   He follows

my strokes   sizes up my splashing   Lung-less

     in the deep long stretches   He eyes my chain

          of blue music

               "You keep swimming

          to your folks and the next ride's on me."

after "Ghost Train" Gethsemane Day

WHERE BLUE LIVES

In the blue lawn

of light; in the blue

of this hidden green

from the cut the lawn

mower brings; prone

on *lawns, while clouds*

fluff past, this blue feeds

our visions of tygers

and lambs. And now

we hear blue *thudding*

above the grass where

insects stand like hairs

on the backs of necks.

Blue can be so wicked.

It gets in everywhere.

It's in our closed lips

now, beneath *the sound*

of wood bumping on wood.

after "The dream-world of my pillow" Gethsemane Day

MY SKIN IS MY GRAVE

Why should dying be news?
The bug is in the matchbox.
The shoebox holds the bird.
The first grave is our backyard.

And Mister Death, the high grotesque,
grins above. Aired in the room
before the earthworms' dark,
lidded and locked, my bones will be

like the cut tree, no longer expanding
in rings. Time skins me, and soon
my *bones will lose their marrow, but they're
brave* disintegrating; being change.

No longer serving their calcified
purpose, *they'll hollow themselves out
for more sonority* and air will song
through them as throats of birds.

after "Bones" Gethsemane Day

LIMESTONE

Here lies the jagged aftermath of pipe-driven
dynamite. Ridges and ledges edge
the scar of a pit. Emptied, gutted,
like a fish and full of water
from veins of hidden springs, what's in me—

always moving. An open
house each season, I absorb
the looking glass of grey, white, black or blue;
the starry source that culls my moods.

I'm passive like a cut
that never heals, only closes
over coldly, a wound of ice and snow.

THERE IS A STIR, ALWAYS

If I hold onto this body the snow will grow inside me
and the winter of my cells will flake
into tiny crystals like six-figured gods,
each arrow tip attempting to make the point of something
as tears flow.

There is a stir, always.

I rise to the cold
to take my place among the fragile stars,
and sleep.

NOTES AND ACKNOWLEDGEMENTS

All italicized words are Dorothy Molloy's.

The poem "Asylum Wall" was inspired by a walking tour led by scholar and activist Geoffrey Reaume of the brick wall surrounding the Centre for Addiction and Mental Health grounds at 1001 Queen Street West during Doors Open Toronto.

~

Versions of some of these poems have appeared in *The Art of Poetic Inquiry Anthology* (Backalong Books), *Branch Magazine, Descant Magazine, Echolocation, Literary Review of Canada, The Malahat Review, The Malahat Review*'s special issue on P.K. Page, *Open Book Toronto*' March Flash Fiction Winner, *The Poet's Quest for God* (forthcoming from Eyewear Publishing), *Prairie Fire, The Puritan, Room Magazine, The Rusty Toque, The Toronto Review of Books* and *Variety Crossing 12th Edition.* My thanks to all the editors.

I am grateful to the Ontario Arts Council for a Writers' Reserve Grant.

Gratitude goes to Noelle Allen at Wolsak & Wynn for providing a beautiful home for my work, to Ashley Hisson for her fine attention to detail and to Natalie Olsen for her stunning book design.

I'd also like to thank James Arthur, Salvatore Difalco, Margot Lettner, A. F. Moritz and Merle Nudelman for their insight on some of the poems during their formative stages; to Ibi Kaslik for her heartwarming friendship and support; to Lois Lorimer for her generous contribution of laughter and literary discourse; to Ian Burgham, poet-comrade-in-arms, for his humour and keen poetic sensibility; and to my friends and family. Lastly, my deepest thanks to Paul Vermeersch for his ongoing faith in my work and, as always, his deft and his exquisite editing.

CATHERINE GRAHAM is the author of four previous poetry collections, including the acclaimed trilogy *Pupa*, *The Red Element* and *Winterkill*. She teaches creative writing at the University of Toronto's School of Continuing Studies, and her poetry has appeared in journals and anthologies around the world. A new and selected volume of her poetry is forthcoming in the United Kingdom. She lives in Toronto.